DATA WITHOUT TEARS

How to Write Measurable Educational Goals and Collect Meaningful Data

Terri Chiara Johnston

Research Press ● 2612 North Mattis Avenue ● Champaign, Illinois 61822
(800) 519-2707 ● www.researchpress.com

RESEARCH PRESS
PUBLISHERS

Copies of this book may be ordered from Research
Press at the address given on the title page.

Cover design by Linda Brown, Positive I.D. Graphic Design, Inc.
Printed by Seaway Printing Co.

ISBN 13: 978-0-87822-627-6
Library of Congress Control Number 2009944073

"Would you tell me, please, which way I ought to go from here?"

"That depends a good deal on where you want to get to," said the Cat.

"I don't much care where," said Alice.

"Then it doesn't matter which way you go," said the Cat.

"As long as I get somewhere," Alice added as an explanation.

"Oh, you're sure to do that," said the Cat, "if you only walk long enough."

—*Alice's Adventures in Wonderland,* Lewis Carroll

Contents

Figures

Acknowledgments

Many people are responsible for this project's becoming a reality. Many thanks go to the "Data Mastermind" group: Sandy Haltrich, Ellen Pochedley, Kim Brush, Kim Peders, Maureen Bartinelli, Karin Fischer-Donovan, and Melissa Higgins. We spent the summer of 2008 eating, drinking, and learning together. The members of this group were the first to put the model into practice. I just ate, drank, and told them what to do. Love you, guys.

Much love and thanks go to my husband, Joe. Apparently, honey, I lied to you. I really didn't retire!

My daughter, Samantha Matthews, and my sister, Rosalee Chiara, and my best friend Sandy Haltrich were my support. Every time I got discouraged, they were the ones who listened and helped me keep going. Throughout my career, Sam has always provided me with good stories to tell about behavior issues! Lee agreed to do the first edit. She e-mailed the draft back and proclaimed, "It's so easy, even a lawyer can do it!" Finally, Sandy has ALWAYS believed in me, even when I didn't! Thanks and love to all of you.

The Brunswick City Schools in Brunswick, Ohio, the Hudson City Schools in Hudson, Ohio, and the Kent City Schools in Kent, Ohio, embarked on the frequently hazardous journey of training their special education staffs to write IEP goals and objectives following the guidelines presented in this document and to collect data efficiently and effectively. It was tough, sometimes stressful, and resulted in MANY "lively" discussions, but we did it! Now some of these teachers who were less than thrilled to be told yet again to change how they do things in their classrooms have become the strongest advocates of the process. Thanks much to the administrators of these fine programs: Dr. Gale Harr, LeeAnn Bailey, and Jinny Widowsky (in Brunswick); Kelly Kemp, Carrie Hutchinson, Doreen Osmun, and Jean Graham-Smith (in Hudson); and Suzanne Frank in Kent, Ohio. Also, thanks to Holly Cifiranic in Hudson for giving me some grassroots credibility when others would have liked to send out a lynch mob!

1

Data: A Four-Letter Word?

Data-Driven Instruction Is Here To Stay

Try walking into any classroom, look into the teacher's eyes, and say just one little word: *data*. No other four-letter word can strike such fear and panic into the heart of an educator. *Data*. If you really want to see some fireworks, try suggesting to teachers that they need to have more and better data collection systems than they currently use. Watch out—excuses, and possibly some objects, will come flying!

Teachers' Top Ten Excuses for Not Collecting Data

1. "You do it! It's a waste of time."
2. "I can't teach and take data at the same time. I'll need an aide."
3. "There aren't enough hours in the day."
4. "There are too many kids and too many objectives."
5. "When will I have time to teach?"
6. "That's not how I do it."
7. "There's too much paperwork already."
8. "I've never had to do this before."
9. "Nobody does it."
10. "It's impossible."

But the most honest response is . . .
"I DON'T KNOW HOW!"

Making the Hardest Job in the World a Little Bit Easier

I have worked with hundreds of educators over my career, serving youngsters who experience mild to severe learning and behavior challenges. Almost to a teacher, they would rather rely on their impressions of a child's performance than struggle with data systems and data collection procedures. Many teachers have excellent intuition, but their impressions and opinions alone won't cut it anymore. Federal and state mandates like the Individuals with Disabilities Education Improvement Act of 2004 (IDEIA) and No Child Left Behind (NCLB) insist that quantitative assessment of progress become standard practice. It is no longer a choice. Collecting and analyzing data in an objective, quantifiable manner is the law.

I believe that teachers have one of the hardest jobs in the world. Not only are they charged with molding the future of humanity, they face all of society's problems (deterioration of family structures, poverty, lack of funds, and so on) before they even get their chance to make a difference in the classroom. The mountains of paperwork they are responsible for, the focus on achievement as defined by standardized tests, and other issues make the work of being an educator extremely challenging.

The sheer number of youngsters who require Individualized Education Programs (IEPs) is astronomical. Each student with an IEP can have as many as ten annual goals with three or four short-term objectives or benchmarks, each requiring quantifiable data management. I refer to IEPs throughout this book, but everything I say about IEPs also relates to the hottest topic in special and general education circles today: Response to Intervention, or RTI. RTI requires early intervention, frequent progress measurement, and increasingly intensive research-based instructional interventions for children who continue to have difficulty. So don't hold your breath anticipating the disappearance of data-driven instruction. The ONLY way this policy is likely to go is toward a demand for MORE data, not less. In fact, if we don't get with the program pretty soon, lawyers and judges will determine the definition of adequate progress, not educators. That, ladies and gentlemen, would be a VERY bad thing.

The task of collecting meaningful data can seem over-whelming, but if you make convenience of data collection and analysis a high priority, it is highly doable. The success of your attempts to collect data on educational goals and objectives depends on two equally important factors:

1. The clarity and completeness of the goals and objectives you write

2. The convenience and practicality of the data collection systems you choose

In this book, I propose a format for writing annual goals and short-term behavior objectives or benchmarks that makes it a snap to collect data. Just follow the **A-B-C-D** steps and the simple guidelines for data collection and you'll be able to:

- Write measurable goals and objectives
- Decide which data collection systems to use to gather mean-ingful information
- Analyze the data you collect and communicate your students' progress accurately
- Make data-based decisions about the effectiveness of inter-ventions and instructional strategies

This book includes multiple examples of common data collec-tion scenarios, but in case you need more, Appendixes A and B provide them. Appendix C includes four basic data collection forms, which you are free to use and adapt to fit your own situa-tion. So hang in there—I've got your back. I not only hope to make this as painless as possible, I am committed to making what I think is the hardest job in the world—your job—just a little bit easier.

Beware of C.R.A.P. Data!

As you read this book, keep in mind that the goal is to gather MEANINGFUL data—not just a bunch of numbers. The only thing worse than no data is what I call C.R.A.P. data, or "Can't Rely on Any Part of It" data. C.R.A.P. data are dangerous. They delude us into believing we can defend our instruction. In truth, however, these data do not represent a reliable measure of progress. Typically, these numbers represent only an attempt to quantify our perceptions of a student's performance.

As an expert witness for school districts who find themselves in due process disputes with parents, it is my job to review all the data that have been collected to document a student's academic or behavioral success, toward the goal of determining the effectiveness of the youngster's program. More often than not, there aren't any data. If there are data, I frequently discover they are not reliable. This creates a big and often expensive problem for the school district. Another common challenge I face is taking a teacher's raw data and trying to summarize it so that it makes sense. In some situations, the raw numbers may look good at first, but a summary and analysis results in the opposite conclusion. This is not a very good position for either the school district or the teacher.

Don't be fooled: C.R.A.P. data are no better than no data at all.

2

If You Don't Know Where You're Going, How Will You Know When You Get There?

Writing Goals That Direct Instruction

IEPs are agreements between families and schools. These agreements include a statement outlining the academic and behavioral changes that the team expects to see in the 12 months that follow—otherwise known as annual goals. These goals are driven by a student's current capabilities, previously learned skills that are prerequisites for achieving new skills, and the rate of progress that can be predicted reasonably based upon knowledge of a student's typical learning performance. Importantly, goals need to be specific, quantifiable, and include a statement defining mastery.

While goals are yearly statements of behavior changes, short-term objectives and benchmarks (also known as progress markers) are used to direct the instruction required to meet the goals and monitor progress toward mastery. Although IDEIA 2004 does not require these progress markers in all situations (see Bateman & Linden, 2006, for a discussion of this issue), I strongly urge maintaining the practice. These progress markers are intended to clarify the plan for teaching the annual goals and provide the IEP team with a prediction of when a student will be able to demonstrate a skill and at what rate of success. Short-term objectives provide a continuity of instruction for a student so that any teacher can provide the proposed instruction. In other words, teachers can be sure that they are teaching the SAME skill in the SAME manner so that a statement of progress can be meaningful. Once evaluated, any adjustments to instruction or interventions can be made.

Think about it this way: I live in a suburb of Cleveland, Ohio. My sister lives in Silver Spring, Maryland, just north of Washington, DC. I visit her several times each year. How do I get there? If I decide to drive, there are several routes I can take. I can drive the Ohio and Pennsylvania Turnpike east (Interstates 80, 76, and 70, which gets me to the Pennsylvania border in about 90 minutes) to Breezewood, Pennsylvania (in about three and a half to four hours depending on the presence of state troopers). I then continue on I-70 east to I-270 to east I-495 (in approximately 90 minutes or so). MapQuest says that's the fastest and easiest, taking about six and a half hours. But I HATE driving the Pennsylvania Turnpike! It's narrow and has a lot of truck traffic. To avoid most of the turnpike, I can go the "southern route," driving just over the Ohio/ Pennsylvania border around Pittsburgh, jumping on I-79 south to Morgantown, West Virginia, and taking I-68 east across the Maryland panhandle to I-70 east, and so on. That takes about seven hours and is much more scenic. Heck, I could drive the back roads, avoiding the turnpikes altogether.

What if I don't want to drive at all? Flying takes just over an hour from Cleveland Hopkins to Baltimore BWI. From home to curbside, it takes just over three hours. What's the best way? It depends on my mood, the weather, the amount of time, construction . . . you name it.

So the difference between annual goals and short-term objectives is this:

- Goals are statements of anticipated changes in a student's behavior within a 12-month period (our destination—in other words, Washington, DC).

- Objectives are the step-by-step directions to get there (the road map or the route I decide to follow).

- Benchmarks designate a date or time increments in progress should be attained (what time I should be at the Ohio/Pennsylvania border, Breezewood, PA, I-270, etc.).

The document describing goals and objectives should be easy to use and provide clear directions to the desired destination. This makes the IEP actually FUNCTIONAL. What a concept!

This is no big revelation to any of us in theory, but in practice too many IEPs are anything but functional. Believe it or not, it is not that unusual for me to read an IEP and conclude that the goals and objectives don't even relate to each other or the present levels of performance statements (PLOPs), which indicate what the student knows and needs to know at the time the IEP is written.

There are a few secrets that make the goal-writing process even easier. Annual goals and associated short-term objectives or benchmarks should be able to stand on their own. What do I mean by that? I mean that as the goals and associated objectives are written, a teacher shouldn't need any additional information to understand WHO the learner is, WHAT needs to be taught, WHERE or in what setting or context the skill should be taught, HOW it should be taught, and WHEN it will be considered mastered.

This is particularly critical when an IEP is written by one team but is to be implemented by another. For instance, it is not uncommon for an IEP to be written in the spring for a fifth-grade student who will transition to middle school in the fall. The elementary team knows the student, knows the student's strengths and weaknesses, and has a good handle on how the student should be instructed in order to be successful. So they write the document. However, in the fall when the middle school folks review the IEP they often scratch their heads, look at each other, shrug, and say, "What the heck were they thinking?" Come on, admit it. This is typical. Even with transition meetings, when somebody else writes the plan, those left to implement it are at a distinct disadvantage.

Ultimately, accountability and a student's response to any academic or behavioral intervention or instruction rely on how well the goal statement is written. Meaningful data start with clearly defined goals (in other words, the destination), but instruction is directed by clearly defined objectives. In other words, once you have agreed upon a student's destination and the route you plan to follow in order to reach it, you should be able to identify ways to collect the data required to evaluate progress.

The notion of a "stand alone" goal and objective is fundamental to making this process work for you. Otherwise, what and how you teach is likely to vary over time and instructors, which means that different evaluators are likely to assess different skills and behaviors, which ultimately results in C.R.A.P. data.

Let's look at some examples. Say that you have a fourth grade youngster who needs to progress in the reading curriculum. You decide he is ready to work on reading comprehension skills. You write the following objective:

> *Johnny will improve his reading comprehension at the*
> *fourth-grade level.*

What does this really mean? Where should you start? What EXACTLY is the problem? Does the student need help with vocabulary, reading orally, reading silently and answering questions, or predicting what happens next in a story? If you don't know WHAT needs fixing, how can he make progress? Do you know where you're going or not?

What about the young lady in your classroom who is considered to be disrespectful and disruptive? What does she do? Does she scream and yell, does she swear at the teacher, or is she talking to her friends during independent work? What exactly does she do that interferes with her learning and the learning of others, and what's your plan to change that?

Years ago, when my daughter was in the third grade, her teacher sent home a note that said, "Samantha needs to learn her multiplication facts. Please work with her at home." I was trained as a teacher, an elementary one at that, so I thought, "No problem. I'll buy some flashcards, and we'll do drills every night for homework." We made it a game, had some fun, and she really got good at responding quickly and accurately when I presented the flashcards. Several weeks passed, and her report card came back with a low math grade and the following note: "Samantha needs to learn her multiplication facts. Please work with her at home." When I spoke to the teacher, she explained that Sam was having trouble understanding simple word problems. But that wasn't what we worked on. In fact, what we spent hours on each week had absolutely nothing to do with word problems!

Writing measurable, "stand alone" goals and objectives is the secret to ending up exactly where you want to be. They tell you WHO, WHAT, WHERE, HOW, and WHEN.

3

It's As Easy As A-B-C-D!

Four Components of a Well-Written Goal

Let's assume we are on the same page now and you're convinced there must be a better way to write goals and objectives. Remember: You must be able to understand and collect data on objectives AS THEY ARE WRITTEN, with no additional information. Let's look at Johnny. Originally, the goal was written as follows:

> *Johnny will improve his reading comprehension at the fourth-grade level.*

Too vague! Improved from what? This goal, as written, doesn't tell us exactly what Johnny needs to do. Let's try it again:

> *Johnny will pass the comprehension section after taking the fourth-grade Metropolitan Achievement Test, scoring 85 percent or better.*

What a difference! We know WHO the learner is, WHAT he's expected to do, HOW he is to do it, and WHEN we'll consider the goal to be mastered. So, our destination is clear, and any observer should be able to agree if Johnny has met the goal or not: Metropolitan Achievement Test, fourth-grade comprehension section, 85 percent.

The destination is set. Now, how do you want to get there? In this case, you really need to describe the "route," so to speak, that you will plot and follow in order to arrive at the destination point. This goal requires short-term objectives to focus in on the skills that Johnny needs. Based on assessment data, does he need instruction in cause and effect analysis, prediction, vocabulary, or something else? Let's say one of the things he has trouble with is predicting what comes next in a story. Here's the first objective for the preceding annual goal, laying out what and how you plan to reach the goal:

> *Johnny will correctly predict what happens next in*
> *writing after listening to a fourth-grade short story four*
> *out of five opportunities over a two-week period.*

In this case, you know WHO the student is (Johnny), you know exactly WHAT you want him to do and HOW (correctly predict what happens next in writing), you know the WHERE or conditions under which you expect to see the behavior (after listening to a fourth-grade short story), and you have identified WHEN it is considered to be mastered (four out of five opportunities over a two-week period.)

I've had great success using the **A-B-C-D** method of writing goals. Dr. Vince Melograno, retired professor at Cleveland State University in the College of Education and Human Services, introduced me to this method at a "trainer of trainers" workshop I attended several years ago (Melograno, 2002). If we break it down, there are four critical components to any goal, objective, or benchmark:

A = AUDIENCE

B = BEHAVIOR

C = CONDITION

D = DEGREE

If you address each component specifically, your goal statement will make data collection simple.

A = Audience

This is the easy part. The **A**, or **Audience**, is the learner or student—the "WHO." Include the youngster's name, and you have part one down pat! Johnny is the audience in the following:

> *Johnny will correctly predict what happens next in writing after listening to a fourth-grade short story four out of five opportunities over a two-week period.*

B = Behavior

This part takes a little more practice. It identifies "WHAT" you want the audience to do. The behavior must be written in terms of visible actions. If it is visible, it can be observed. If it is observed, it can be counted. If it can be counted, it can be summarized. If it can be summarized, it can be evaluated.

The **B** for **Behavior** in this model includes the specific actions that the youngster is to perform, demonstrate, or exhibit. Describe WHAT you want the youngster to do. For example, you want him to "complete all assignments" or "follow two-step directions" or "remain in designated area" or "count orally to 100," and so on. The target behavior should be so clear that a person who does not know the youngster is able to determine whether the student is demonstrating the behavior. Generally speaking, you are looking for the student to INCREASE the number of times the behavior occurs (in other words, frequency) or decrease the number of times the behavior occurs (also frequency), or you want to determine whether a specific outcome has or has not transpired.

In my experience, writing solid behavior descriptions is the hardest part of the process for teachers. When I ask teachers, "Tell me exactly what you want your student to do," with encouragement, they can tell me pretty clearly. Writing it down, however, is a different matter. This takes practice and is best learned working and getting feedback from others. Eventually, it becomes second nature. Once learned, teachers are excited about this format because it leads directly to strategies for effective instruction.

The behavior in the following is "will correctly predict what happens next in writing":

> Johnny <u>will correctly predict what happens next in writing</u> after listening to a fourth-grade short story four out of five opportunities over a two-week period.

This **B** for **Behavior** statement not only tells you what you want Johnny to do (predicting what comes next), it also describes exactly how you expect him to do it (in writing). Just writing "will correctly predict what happens next" isn't enough in and of itself. Making it clear that you want a written product is necessary. Otherwise, folks could accept an oral statement. If an oral response is sufficient, a very different procedure for collecting data will be required. Instead of a paper product that you can evaluate anytime at your leisure, oral answers require direct observation at the time Johnny is reading and predicting. That means that somebody has to be there right then to document his performance of the skill. This may or may not be convenient or even possible to do.

Some examples of behavior descriptions follow in Figure 1. The difference between column one and two is specificity. If three people observed a youngster engaged in an instructional activity, most likely they could agree whether the student demonstrated the behavior outcomes listed in column two, but there could be three different opinions as to whether the student met expectations as defined in column one. Examples like the ones in the second column are sufficient for skills you wish to increase. When you need to clearly define challenging behaviors that you wish to *decrease,* an additional step, identifying "Start Time and Stop Time," is required. We'll save that discussion for Chapter 7.

FIGURE 1 Behavior Descriptions

Vague Behavior Statements	Clear Behavior Statements
Will understand money concepts.	Will orally count nickels, dimes, and quarters up to $2.
Will improve written expression.	Will write a paragraph containing 100 words or more.
Will demonstrate appropriate social skills.	Will look at the speaker when greeting the person.
Will understand the difference between two similar objects.	Will verbalize the differences between two similar objects, (e.g., a red circle and a red square, a brown bear and a black bear, etc.).
Will recognize size.	Will identify size differences by pointing to a small, medium, or large item.
Will be successful in a sixth-grade social studies course.	Will earn a grade of C or better.
Will make wise choices when upset.	Will choose and demonstrate a self-calming plan from a list of pre-learned and practiced strategies.

C = Condition

Condition, or C, refers to the context in which you expect the student to perform the new skill or reduce the occurrence of the problem behavior. Here is where a teacher can list the special materials a student may need (calculator, picture cards, word bank, vocabulary list, and so forth) or special supports like the number or type of prompts that should be made available (two verbal prompts, one gestural prompt, physical assistance, and so on). For the most part, the conditions, or "givens," need to be clearly spelled out in the goals and objectives so there is no question about what is necessary for instruction. Conditions can involve the triggers, cues, antecedents, particular settings or times of day, and so on that set the stage for the target behavior or skill to occur—for example, "After a verbal direction," "Given written instructions," "Upon entering the classroom," "During independent work," and "After listening to a lecture."

What's the condition statement in the following example?

> *Johnny will correctly predict what happens next in writing <u>after listening to a fourth-grade short story</u> four out of five opportunities over a two-week period.*

You're right if you said "after listening to a fourth-grade short story."

In another example, you may be teaching a student a particular morning arrival routine so she can be independent when coming into the classroom, putting her belongings in the proper area, and starting her seat work. It only makes sense that you expect the youngster to perform these steps in the MORNING, before class officially begins. By providing the phrase "Upon entering the classroom in the morning . . . " you make it clear not only that it is at that time you expect the behavior to occur but also that it will be at that time you will evaluate the student's performance.

Often teachers want a student to refrain from talking out in class. The condition statement helps define the context in which the behavior should occur. Consider the objective statement "Teddy will raise his hand to speak." A statement like this is way too ambiguous. Throughout any school day, there are many situations in which students would never be expected to raise their hands before speaking. For example, at lunch raising a hand to speak to friends would be ridiculous. Context affects what rules a youngster needs to follow and when. The objective would be clearer if written like this:

> *Teddy will raise his hand before speaking when listening to a story at circle time.*

Or like this:

> *During a class lecture, Teddy will raise his hand before speaking.*

In these examples, when you expect a student to raise a hand prior to talking out and where you will collect the data for this behavior are very clear. Being this clear is also a strategy that helps Teddy understand when it's okay to talk and when it isn't.

Other conditions may include the type of assistance or supports that will be provided in order to increase the likelihood of the student's success. If the student needs extra prompting before being able to demonstrate the behavior, it's important to identify what type and how many prompts you feel will be necessary. Levels of prompts from most to least include (but are not limited to) the following:

- Full physical prompts, which involve hand-over-hand guidance or actually moving a youngster's body in order to perform the behavior.

- Partial physical prompts, which are a reduction of the amount of physical support provided.

- Gestural prompts, which occur when the teacher gestures toward the correct choice.

- Verbal prompts, meaning an additional verbal cue or reminder is given so the youngster will respond.

I have seen teachers use the phrase "with faded prompts" to indicate an expectation that during initial instruction several prompts will be provided, but the number and type of prompts will be reduced over time. I believe that this is not clear enough and violates the rule that objectives must be understandable as they are written, with no additional information. In evaluating the objective, there is no way to know what "faded" really means. Are we fading from ten to five prompts, from full physical prompting to gestural prompts, or from gestural prompts to verbal prompts?

The condition statement can be placed in order (Audience-Behavior-**Condition**-Degree), but the goal or objective often reads better if the condition statement is written first (**Condition**-Audience-Behavior-Degree), as in this example:

> *Given a list of third-grade spelling words, Carl will spell the words on weekly spelling tests averaging 85 percent accuracy in a 10-week grading period.*

Sometimes it sounds better to break up the condition statement when listing a number of needed "givens" (**Condition**-Audience-Behavior-**Condition**-Degree), as in the following:

> *During independent work sessions, Missy will complete four work activities with no more than two verbal reminders four out of five consecutive work sessions.*

Bateman and Herr (2006) say that there are occasions when the "givens," or conditions, are obvious or implied and do not need to be listed. I disagree. I think it is important to maintain a consistent format in order to be absolutely sure nothing of importance is missed and the statement can stand alone. I strongly urge you to include a condition statement for each goal and objective you write.

Following are some examples of where, when, and what materials and prompts may be needed for a youngster to be successful:

- During circle time with one verbal reminder
- Given the manual sign for toilet and a partial physical prompt
- On the playground

- When provided a calculator
- In the gym
- During transition from one activity to another and with one gestural prompt toward the child's posted schedule
- During independent work time
- Given a worksheet with 20 problems
- Presented with a choice of three
- Given a model
- After a lecture
- Upon completion of an activity
- After reading an assigned story
- Given a diagram
- Upon completion of an activity and with no more than one verbal reminder
- When given a picture communication book and two or fewer gestural prompts
- Given a visual cue
- With partial physical assistance
- Throughout the school setting (This is a very generic "given" that you can use when there are no other particular context or support statements needed.)

D = Degree

The last piece of the puzzle is **D** for **Degree**, also known as criteria. An effective goal or objective needs to state clearly what is considered to be acceptable performance:

> *Johnny will correctly predict what happens next in writing after listening to a fourth-grade short story <u>four out of five opportunities over a two-week period.</u>*

Many teachers state degrees in terms of percentages. Percentages work well when you can clearly count, observe, or measure 100 percent of something—for example, if you are grading a test or any other assignment that involves a finite total amount. Percentages don't typically work for behavioral observation data. In other words, if you can't possibly observe a student 100 percent of a school day, you can't write a degree statement that sets mastery level as 80 percent of the school day. The "total" or "100 percent" MUST be a fixed total amount so that it is possible to calculate a portion of that amount. Remember: If you can't count ALL of it, you can't calculate a percentage.

For example, suppose you have a youngster who presents a challenging behavior. How, where, and when would you be able to collect data on the following objective?

> *Donna will follow classroom rules 80 percent of the time.*

It would be impossible to calculate a percentage of the entire day. First of all, you would need a measurable behavior statement that clarifies exactly what "will follow classroom rules" looks like. Also, it is critical to list where or when you are most interested in having Donna be better at following the rules.

Identifying in the goal or objective where she has the most trouble would be an excellent setting in which to evaluate whether she is improving or not. For example:

> *<u>During transitions between activities,</u> Donna will reduce the number of times she touches, grabs, kicks, or otherwise physically engages another student to zero, 80 percent of designated observation periods.*

Here you have specified what you expect to see (or not see) and when and where you will watch and evaluate the behavior (in other words, the condition statement "during transitions between activities"). With a goal statement like this, it is not only possible to collect meaningful data, the results can be expressed as a ratio or percentage (number of observations in which the behavior did occur out of the total number of observation periods).

Other examples of degree statements include the following:

- Number correct
- Fifteen out of 20 correct responses
- Within a five-minute time period
- Label all 10 items correctly
- With 85 percent accuracy across all observation periods
- On 80 percent of opportunities
- All 20 problems answered correctly
- Four out of five trials correct
- On five consecutive trials
- Complete all steps

I personally like to include a "consecutive time" phrase in the degree statement. This way you can be pretty sure that mastery can be sustained. If you use a simple phrase like "4/5 opportunities" or trials, technically, mastery occurs the first time the student achieves the 4/5 criteria. If I ask a teacher, "Once he's done it four out of five times, do you think he has really mastered the skill?" the teacher says no. Therefore, I like adding the phrase "over two (three, four, whatever) consecutive weeks" to be very sure the skill is mastered and will be maintained.

It has not been my practice to attach a specific date predicting when the objective will be met. I see that as more of a "benchmark" notation. Some supervisors and state oversight agencies require this. I feel it means if you don't meet the specific date, you don't meet the objective. However, not everybody sees it my way, so you must check with your district supervisor to be sure you're complying. With a specific date added, Johnny's example would look like this:

Johnny will correctly predict what happens next in writing after listening to a fourth-grade short story four out of five opportunities over a two week period <u>by the end of the first grading period.</u>

If you understand the **A-B-C-D's** of writing measurable goals and objectives, collecting meaningful data can be a piece of cake. Congratulations! Take a deep breath. You're almost ready to take data.

4

K.I.S.S. Me!

Keeping Data Simple

There is another issue I need to address that is typical of educators: We tend to want to collect data on EVERYTHING! We try to document too many things—what a student does, when, how much, how, with whom, what came first, what came last, what the student didn't do, what the student should have done . . . you get the picture.

The key here is K.I.S.S.—Keep It Simple Sweetheart!

There may be a thousand little things about a student's performance that would be interesting to know, but capturing them in a reliable, quantifiable manner is impossible. On the other hand, you may think of a great way to document variables, but if you have too many things to record, it may take longer to fill out the data sheets than it does to instruct the youngster! No wonder teachers get frustrated and overwhelmed. Remember K.I.S.S.: Only collect data on what is absolutely necessary. Otherwise, you'll make yourself crazy!

For example, what if your objective is written like this:

> *Given a model (Condition), Marie (Audience) will write the uppercase letters of the alphabet (Behavior) without errors four out of five consecutive opportunities (Degree).*

All you REALLY need to assess is whether Marie is writing uppercase letters without errors when she has a model to look at. That's it! Yes she did, or no she didn't. All other concerns, such as which letters she knows and which she doesn't, which letters are written but need to be neater, whether she writes them in order or out of order, and on and on need not be formally documented. These are concerns in which teacher observations and impressions are sufficient.

The preceding objective tells you by the way it is written exactly WHAT you need to count and WHEN you should count it. First, you collect data ONLY when Marie is given the model. Second, you continue to collect data until she has completed the task without errors for four out of five consecutive opportunities. Third, she must write all 26 letters correctly. That's it! That's all! You're done!

The Dirty Little Secret to Making It Work

In order for data systems to be convenient, goals and objectives need to be written clearly and concisely. As written, these statements should outline exactly how they are to be evaluated. As I said in Chapter 3, there are four critical components to a well-written objective. If you address each one specifically, data collection can be simple:

A = AUDIENCE, or who will demonstrate the behavior

B = BEHAVIOR, or exactly what you want the audience to do or not do

C = CONDITION, or where, when, and what supports you will provide to the audience to increase the likelihood that the behavior will occur

D = DEGREE, or the criteria you have set that will indicate the youngster has mastered the behavior

The purpose of writing objectives in the **A-B-C-D** format is to make this process not only much easier but also more convenient. Here's the dirty little secret to making this work for you:

1. Write your goal and objectives to answer the question "Did the student demonstrate the behavior, or didn't he?" The youngster is evaluated merely by marking either "Yes/No" or "Correct/ Incorrect." If you do this, you can use a limited number of data collection formats for almost any goal or objective you need to assess.

2. Once you've written an objective, design the data collection method and data collection form IMMEDIATELY. If you find you can't figure out a way to collect data conveniently and accurately, REWRITE THE OBJECTIVE!

I really can't emphasize this enough. By writing goal and objective statements with data collection in mind, you'll save yourself a lot of headaches when the time comes for designing instructional strategies, teaching the skills, and documenting progress.

5

A Bird in the Hand . . .

Permanent Products and Quantified Behavior Observations

In general, there are only two acceptable data collection methods for evaluating instruction and intervention effectiveness:

1. Reviewing and evaluating permanent products that sample a student's knowledge or achievement
2. Conducting quantified observations of behaviors

Qualitative narratives and teacher impressions fall in the C.R.A.P. data category—in other words, Can't Rely on Any Part of It). Figure 2 summarizes the accuracy of these three methods.

Let's review the two collection methods that actually work.

Permanent Products

The most common type of data teachers take are grades. Typically, you are evaluating or grading a paper or the result of an activity or task, including worksheets, reports, tests, quizzes, and so on that include right and wrong answers. Whenever possible, this is the way to go. You are using concrete products, a "bird in the hand" as it were, that do not require direct observation of the student's performance. The product itself can be evaluated and the data recorded whenever you have the time.

FIGURE 2   Data Collection Methods for Evaluating Response to Intervention

Permanent Products	• Most accurate and most convenient. • Generally, there is a right and wrong answer. • Use whenever possible.
Quantified Behavior Observations	• Generally accurate and reasonably convenient IF carefully designed. • Behavior descriptions should be written so there is only one correct response.
Qualitative Narratives or Teacher Impressions	• C.R.A.P. data! • Unreliable: Two instructors could easily disagree on whether a response is correct or incorrect. • DO NOT USE AS A PRIMARY DATA SOURCE. Can be used to supplement quantified data.

Your data for the following objective will consist of grading Jake's worksheets:

> *Given a worksheet (Condition), Jake (Audience) will label, in writing, all of the nouns and verbs (Behavior) with 85 percent accuracy over four consecutive assignments (Degree).*

You grade the paper and report performance in the form of percentage correct. Jake either did label all the nouns and verbs, or he missed some. Black and white, yes or no. The data shown in Figure 3 are summarized by graphing the result of each worksheet. One look at the graph of Jake's grades (Figure 4) shows that he not only made progress but is close to mastering the objective. In other words, your instruction is working.

FIGURE 3 Jake's Grade Data

	Worksheet									
	1	2	3	4	5	6	7	8	9	10
Grade	45%	59%	69%	79%	65%	79%	81%	89%	91%	100%

FIGURE 4 Graph of Jake's Grade Data

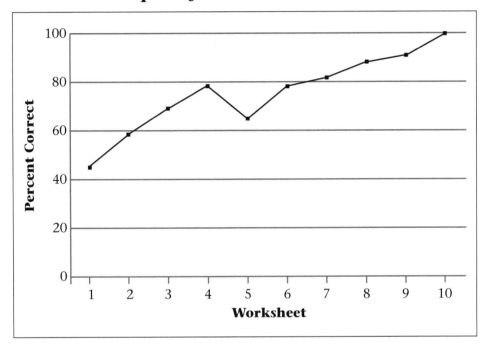

Figure 5 shows some other examples of objectives assessed using permanent products. Each task requires the learner to write a response. The teacher is able to evaluate that response, which is in the form of a worksheet, when it is convenient. Also, the worksheet can be kept as a work sample.

Quantified Behavior Observations

You can use this same format when evaluating the outcome of a task or activity that is not in a written form but does exist in some other tangible form. Consider this objective:

FIGURE 5   Objectives Assessed with Permanent Products: Worksheets or Tests

Audience	Behavior	Condition	Degree
AJ	will complete the spelling test	when given a third-grade spelling word list	Earning a grade of 85% or better 8/10 weekly tests
David	will write all the uppercase numbers of the alphabet	when prompted by his teacher	in correct order with no more than 3 errors 9/10 opportunities
Carol	will write the correct time to the nearest 5 minutes	given a clock face with the hands in any position	9/10 opportunities
Ben	will write a story containing at least 10 complete sentences	given a starter phrase	with no more than 5 total errors in spelling, punctuation, or grammer in 4/5 stories

Given a choice of 20 items which include three different colors (red, blue, green) (Condition), Tommy (Audience) will manually sort the items by three different colors (Behavior) without assistance and without errors nine out of ten opportunities (Degree).

Once the task is completed, it remains intact until the teacher has an opportunity to "grade" it. The raw data consist of a record of the number of items Tommy sorted correctly. He either sorted three different colors correctly with no errors, or he didn't. All or nothing. Although the outcome of his sorting is not a permanent product that will be saved as a sample, it is still a "product" or "outcome" of the youngster's behavior. It can stay as the youngster created it until the teacher evaluates his performance. Then the raw data are recorded on a form and can be summarized.

As you can see in Figure 6, out of 10 designated opportunities between October 9 and November 10, Tommy has only sorted all 20 items correctly twice. That was easy. Two out of 10 opportunities correct. He's not close to mastering this objective. That's the science of teaching. What about the art? Should you change directions in instructional strategies or not? Well, that depends upon your QUALITATIVE data. How close is Tommy to getting all 20 correct? What is your error analysis? Is there a problem, or is this just going to take some time? THAT is what teacher observations are for. Writing comments about Tommy's progress or approach to the task supplements your quantitative data and can help you choose different teaching methods. The data alone tell you there has been minimal progress in the past 30 days.

FIGURE 6   **Tommy's Sorting Performance**

Behavior: Sort three colors correctly

10/9	10/14	10/22	10/25	10/30	10/31	11/2	11/5	11/7	11/10
Yes / (No)	Yes / (No)	Yes / (No)	Yes / (No)	Yes / (No)	Yes / (No)	(Yes)/ No	Yes / (No)	(Yes)/ No	Yes / (No)

Each of the examples in Figure 7 provides a tangible artifact, product, or environmental effect that can be viewed and rated by the teacher when it's convenient. Product data are the easiest and most defensible type of data teachers can collect. Whenever possible, write all your objectives with this data collection method in mind.

FIGURE 7   Objectives Assessed with Observed Outcomes

Audience	Behavior	Condition	Degree
Oscar	will tie his shoes without assistance	when asked to put on his shoes	100% of observed opportunities for 4 consecutive weeks
Eddie	will place the hands of an analog clock in the correct position within 5 minutes	when asked, "Eddie, show me _____ o'clock"	4/5 requests over 2 consecutive weeks
Brian	will match the correct picture to the corresponding word	when given picture cards and corresponding word labels	9/10 trials over 3 consecutive weeks
Carlos	will assemble no fewer than 25 packages in 30 minutes	when given a 5-item assembly job	in 4/5 designated observations

6

If At First You Don't Succeed, Trial, Trial Again

Increasing Desired Behaviors

Many IEP objectives do not lend themselves to product grading, discussed in the last chapter. Here's an example:

> *When requested (Condition), Mary (Audience) will verbally count from 1 to 20 (Behavior) without prompts (Condition) with 100 percent accuracy for five consecutive days (Degree).*

In this case the **B** or **Behavior** is counting out loud from 1 to 20. This requires a teacher to witness the behavior being demonstrated and record the performance immediately. In order for behaviors to be observable and measurable, they must be defined specifically and in a way that the event or occurrence of that behavior has a DISCRETE beginning and ending. In Mary's case, she starts counting at 1 and counts all the numbers between 1 and 20, in sequence, out loud, ending at 20.

Collecting observation data is the biggest stumbling block for most teachers. Remember, one of the two critical factors in data keeping is making data collection convenient (K.I.S.S.)! (The other is writing clear objectives.) Data must be EASY to access and record. For the most part, teachers attempt to take frequency data in the form of recording EACH AND EVERY EVENT THAT OCCURS. This works whether you want to increase or decrease a behavior. It is the most exact and potentially accurate way of communicating the extent to which the target behavior or skill is demonstrated. Think carefully about committing yourself to recording each and every event, however. If the rate or frequency of behavior is too high, it may not be possible to count and record each event accurately. We'll discuss alternatives to event recording in Chapter 8.

To INCREASE behavior, the first step is identifying which of four behavior dimensions you want to influence or change:

1. Frequency (or rate)
2. Duration
3. Latency
4. Intensity

Again, K.I.S.S.—Keep It Simple Sweetheart! Don't be tempted to keep data on several dimensions at the same time. It will be extremely difficult to collect accurate data across multiple dimensions. If you attempt to do this, you end up with C.R.A.P. data. Choose the most critical dimension first and see if you feel it gives you adequate information for evaluation.

Let's look at a form you'd use to record Mary's "counting" behavior (Figure 8). Here's the objective again:

> *When requested (Condition), Mary (Audience) will*
> *verbally count from 1 to 20 (Behavior) without prompts*
> *(Condition) with 100 percent accuracy for five*
> *consecutive days (Degree).*

As shown, you just fill in the date and circle "Yes" if Mary verbally counts from 1 to 20 accurately or "No" if she doesn't. You can summarize the data by providing the percentage of days she counted correctly by dividing the "Yeses" by the "Nos." In Mary's case, she counted correctly 67 percent of the days.

FIGURE 8   **Mary's Counting Behavior**

	Date								
	1/5	1/7	1/9	1/12	1/18	1/25	1/30	2/3	2/6
Counted with 100% accuracy	Yes / (No)	Yes / (No)	(Yes)/ No	(Yes)/ No	Yes / (No)	(Yes)/ No	(Yes)/ No	(Yes)/ No	(Yes)/ No

The following data collection format is a basic example of the one I recommend the most. It is designed for any observational objective that can be evaluated with a "Yes/No" or "Correct/Incorrect" designation. The best part is that it is "self-graphing." You can modify it anyway you'd like. Here's how it works.

ITEMS: You list the individual items, parts, or steps required when demonstrating a skill (or just a behavior description). For example, if you want a student to spell a list of ten words correctly out loud, list all the words in the "Item" column. If you are teaching a multistep routine or task, such as getting ready for lunch, washing hands, or completing a vocational job, these steps can be written in the "Item" column. If there is a sequence to the skill be sure to write the first step in row "1", second in "2," and so forth.

1–10 COLUMNS: Starting from number "1," if the student responds correctly, you circle the item number. If not, you put an X through the number. At the end of the session, you count the number of circles (correct responses) and place a box around the numeral that corresponds to the number the youngster got correct.

After several sessions, you need only connect the boxes, thereby graphing the student's progress over the number of sessions.

The following example requires Ben to demonstrate a behavior immediately after a cue (S^{d}, demand, direction, and so on). Check out his progress on the following objective:

> *When given the instruction "Give me (various objects such as ball, toy, spoon)" (Condition), Ben (Audience) will pick up the object and hand it to the instructor (Behavior) four out of five times over three consecutive sessions (Degree).*

As you can see in Figure 9, the first session on October 14, Ben only responded correctly one time, which was on the third item. The teacher noted the correct response by circling number four, "pencil." Ben responded incorrectly to all the other items, and the teacher put an *X* through those numbers. The total of correct responses, one, is noted by placing a box around the number 1. Each instructional session is noted in the same way. On November 8, the boxes are connected, and the resulting graph indicates Ben is coming close to meeting the criteria of four out of five in three consecutive sessions.

You can give this data sheet to an assistant who can implement the instruction exactly as you have written it. The assistant is able

FIGURE 9   Ben's Item Identification Using Self-Graphing Data Form

Dates	10/14	10/17	10/20	10/25	10/26	10/28	10/31	11/4	11/5	11/8
Session	1	2	3	4	5	6	7	8	9	10
5. Square	X	X	X	X	X	X	X	X	X	X
4. Pencil	④	④	④	④	④	④	[④]	[④]	④	[④]
3. Truck	X	X	X	[③]	③	[③]	③	③	[X]	③
2. Spoon	X	X	[X]	X	[X]	X	②	②	②	②
1. Ball	[X]	[X]	①	①	X	①	①	①	①	①

to take data easily and quickly, and graphing is immediate. What more could you ask for?

To use this format, just make sure the goal or objective statement is EXACTLY what you want the youngster to do in very discrete terms. Then it becomes a very black and white decision and recording is easy: Did the behavior occur, or didn't it? K.I.S.S.— Keep It Simple Sweetheart!

The following example can be used when the skill or task you want the youngster to perform has several steps or items that never change: a task analysis, a spelling word list, a list of words to read aloud, and so forth. For example, if you're teaching Emily to wash her hands without assistance, you are likely to design a task analysis for "handwashing." The objective might look like this:

> *Given a task analysis for handwashing (Condition),*
> *Emily (Audience) will complete the routine to wash and*
> *dry her hands (Behavior) with one or fewer errors 9 out*
> *of 10 designated observations (Degree).*

Figure 10 shows the 10-step task analysis, listed in reverse order. You score this the same as Mary's counting objective and Ben's item identification objective. As you can see, it's easy to graph progress immediately. Lots of objectives lend themselves to this quick and easy data collection method. Figure 11 includes several more examples.

FIGURE 10   Emily's Task Analysis for Hand Washing Using Self-Graphing Data Form

	Session				
Steps	1	2	3	4	5
10. Throws towel away	✗10	✗10	✗10	⑩	⑩
9. Dries hands	✗	✗	✗	✗	✗
8. Gets paper towel	✗	✗	✗	✗	✗
7. Turns water off	⑦	⑦	⑦	⑦	⑦
6. Rinses hands	✗	✗	✗	✗	✗
5. Lathers backs of hands	✗	✗	✗	✗	✗
4. Lathers palms	✗	✗	✗	☒	☒
3. Puts soap on hands	✗	☒	☒	✗	✗
2. Wets hands	☒	②	②	②	②
1. Turns water on	①	①	①	①	①

FIGURE 11   Sample Objectives Compatible with Self-Graphing Format

Audience	Behavior	Condition	Degree
Sally	will balance on one foot for 5 seconds retaining her balance without falling	when requested	for 4/5 designated opportunities
Andrew	will recite the poem	after memorizing a poem assigned by his teacher	with fewer than 3 errors 4/5 designated opportunities
Michael	will verbally retell the story in proper sequence	after listening to a short story	4/5 designated opportunities
Susan	will solve the problem "in her head" without paper and pencil	given a fifth-grade level math story problem presented orally	correctly 9/10 designated opportunities
Danny	will count various amounts of change up to $1	given quarters, dimes, and nickles	9/10 trials
Moe	will count 20 objects using 1:1 correspondence	upon request	with 100% accuracy 4/5 designated opportunities
Karen	will imitate the action	given the direction "Karen, do this ____"	within 3 seconds 9/10 designated opportunities

7

It's All In the Eyes of the Beholder

Decreasing Challenging Behavior

For the most part, when a teacher complains about a kid's behavior, he or she finds a behavior to be occurring at an unacceptable rate. In other words, the objective is to DECREASE the occurrence of the target behavior. This may mean reducing the frequency to a more acceptable level or extinguishing the behavior altogether.

The "shape" of a behavior—also known as the topography or the description—is unique to each youngster. What I mean is, although you might label two students' behavior as aggression, the words you use to describe what aggression "looks like" for each student are not the same.

Remember in Chapter 3 we said that when we use a behavior observation method of data collection, the behavior MUST be a DISCRETE event? That means the behavior must either result in a finished product OR have a distinct beginning and ending. I call this the "Start Time" and the "Stop Time," and this additional information is a critical factor when quantifying excessive behavior so that you can reliably count how often it occurs. To be sure that you have described a behavior clearly and that it has a discrete beginning and ending, have three colleagues read your description, with "Start" and "Stop" times defined, and ask them to observe the student. If they can all agree when the behavior occurs—that is, when it starts and when it stops— you're golden!

To show you how different definitions of behavior can be, let's look at Billy and Toby's aggressive behavior.

Billy's Aggression

Description: Punching another individual with a closed fist several times with such force as to leave bruises.

Start/Stop Time: Aggression starts when Billy makes contact with another individual in an aggressive manner, as defined above, and it stops when Billy is no longer in physical contact with that individual for 15 minutes or more.

Toby's Aggression

Description: Open hand raised above his head, coming down in a "slapping" motion, typically making contact with an adult's shoulder with minimal force.

Start/Stop Time: Aggression starts when Toby makes contact with the adult in an aggressive manner, as defined above, and ends when he removes his hand from the adult's shoulder.

Okay, you tell me. If you had to choose being hit by Billy or Toby, whose aggression would be the most tolerable? Toby's, of course, because the result of his aggression would be annoyance, not pain or bruises. It would be over immediately, whereas Billy's attack could last several minutes.

Some other definitions of aggression are listed in Figure 12. Remember, it's all about what the youngster DOES that you consider aggressive. Each description can certainly be labeled aggression, but the "shape" or "topography" of each one is quite different. Keep in mind that the behavior description includes ONLY what the youngster does when being aggressive. It does NOT include why you think a student engages in the behavior, such as "Tommy becomes aggressive when he is told no" or "When Colleen is frustrated, she becomes aggressive." You use ONLY words that describe the physical characteristics of the behavior.

FIGURE 12 Examples of Definitions for Aggression

Descriptions	Start and Stop Time
Example 1	
Hitting, kicking, spitting, screaming, and otherwise causing pain/discomfort to another individual	**START:** Behavior is considered started when any of the descriptors occur.
	STOP: Behavior is considered stopped when the youngster is calm and following a teacher's direction for 5 minutes or more.
Example 2	
Biting another person, leaving a bruise or puncturing the skin	**START:** Behavior starts when the youngster's mouth makes any kind of contact with another person.
	STOP: Behavior stops when there is no longer any physical contact with the youngster's mouth.
Example 3	
Pinching, pushing, or scratching another person	**START:** Behavior is considered started when any of the descriptors occurs.
	STOP: Behavior stops when any of the descriptors no longer occurs for 15 seconds or more.

Overt behaviors such as hitting, spitting, crying, screaming, and so on are relatively easy to define. However, what about more nebulous issues like "noncompliance," "off task," or "disrespect"? Just like aggression, these behaviors require a teacher to describe exactly what a student LOOKS like when he or she is noncompliant, off task, or disrespectful. That can sometimes be a big problem for educators.

Think of a student that you've had in your class you instantly considered disrespectful. What did this student DO that was disrespectful? Did she roll her eyes at you? Did she call you names, like "stupid," "fatty," or "bitch"? Again, it is important to define the challenging behaviors in such a way that anybody observing would pretty much agree that the behavior was or was not occurring. I often add a statement in a behavior description that includes examples of what the student does. See if you can get a picture of what these kids actually DO.

Molly's Noncompliance

Description: Failure to follow a teacher's direction within 60 seconds.

Start/Stop Time: Noncompliance starts 60 seconds after a teacher gives Molly a direction and she does not comply, and it stops once Molly has followed the direction and continues to comply for five minutes or more.

Artie's Disrespect

Description: Verbalizations characterized by foul language or oppositionality, making statements such as "I don't have to do this," or "I hate you," "You bitch," and "F ___ you."

Start/Stop Time: Disrespect starts when Artie uses foul language or statements like the ones listed above and stops once Artie is following a teacher's direction and is engaged in the assigned activity for 30 minutes or more.

Carter's Off-Task Behavior

Description: Any behavior exhibited that is not related to assigned task or activity (for example, talking with peers, disrupting peer activities, wandering the room, and leaving the classroom).

Start/Stop Time: Off-task behavior starts when Carter is not engaged in the assigned activity as just defined and stops when he is engaged in the assigned task for three minutes or more.

The Start Time makes sense, but why does the Stop Time indicate that Carter must be on task for three minutes or more? Why did I say Molly is considered to be compliant only after five minutes? Why do I want 30 minutes or more to pass before I consider Artie back on track? The simple answer is this: I know these kids. I know that Artie could easily erupt again if I am fooled into thinking he's calm once he says he is. I would be counting one discrete incident as numerous events when, in actuality, it is all the same one. In other words, I don't consider the problem over until I'm certain, based upon my experience and knowledge of each individual student.

Again, the behavior description is dependent upon what each individual student DOES that is considered to be a problem behavior that needs to be eliminated or decreased. It is up to the team to decide the Start and Stop Time. Without it, you can't measure frequency.

If the behavior occurs no more often than once, twice, or three times an hour and doesn't last a long time, a great way of documenting it is to use a grid, or "scatter plot," like the one filled out for Jason (Figure 13). The documentation intervals can be structured in any way that is convenient—for example, class periods (first, second, third, and so on) or activity contexts (circle time, math time, and so forth). You're interested in seeing when and where the behavior occurs. Each time the target behavior occurs, you put a hash mark in the appropriate time slot. You then add up the tallies at the end of each day. The data can then be graphed (Figure 14).

The critical factor here is this: EVERY OCCURRENCE OF THE BEHAVIOR MUST BE DOCUMENTED WITHIN MINUTES OF THE INCIDENT! If you wait, you're likely to rely on memory as to the

FIGURE 13   Jason's Scatter Plot for "Out of Area" Behavior

Period	Class	Monday	Tuesday	Wednesday	Thursday	Friday
1st	Home-room					
2nd	Math					
3rd	Reading	//	/	/	/	/
4th	Specials			/		
5th	Lunch					
6th	Science		///	/	/	/
7th	Writing					
8th	World literature	//	//	/		//
9th	Band					
	Totals	**4**	**6**	**4**	**2**	**4**

FIGURE 14   Graph of Jason's "Out of Area" Behavior

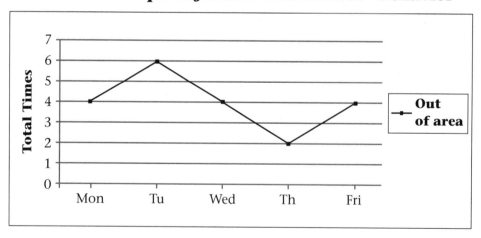

frequency, underestimating or overestimating its occurrence. Recording every occurrence sounds easy enough, but it can be really tricky. I have seen teachers use paperclips in pockets to note behavior occurrences as they happen, transferring a clip from one pocket to another to count or keep track of the events. Later, they count the number of paperclips transferred and note the number in the appropriate time slot. Other ideas include putting a strip of masking tape on a sleeve and making tally marks on that, using tokens in a jar on a desk, using a small counter, and folding a piece of paper in half each time the behavior occurs. At the end of the designated interval, the number of occurrences is noted. At the end of the day, a total for the day is recorded.

So, let's take the example of Jason. He is "out of area" during the school day, as defined in the following way.

Jason's Out of Area Behavior

Description: Removing himself entirely from the physical space he is assigned to for 30 seconds or more.

Start/Stop Time: The behavior starts at the point Jason is outside of his assigned physical space for more than 30 seconds. The behavior stops when Jason returns to his assigned physical space for five minutes or more.

I can use the scatter plot format to collect baseline data and determine an average number of times Jason is "out of area." Once baseline is collected, a behavior goal and associated objectives can be written:

> *Throughout the school day (Condition), Jason*
> *(Audience) will reduce his "out of area" behavior (see*
> *definition, baseline is 4 times a day) (Behavior) to zero*
> *for four consecutive weeks (Degree).*

Benchmark 1: Throughout the school day (Condition), Jason (Audience) will reduce his "out of area" behavior (see definition)

(Behavior) to three times a day for two consecutive weeks (Degree).

Benchmark 2: Throughout the school day (Condition), Jason (Audience) will reduce his "out of area" behavior (see definition) (Behavior) to two times a day for two consecutive weeks (Degree).

Benchmark 3: Throughout the school day (Condition), Jason (Audience) will reduce his "out of area" behavior (see definition) (Behavior) to one time a day for two consecutive weeks (Degree).

Benchmark 4: Throughout the school day (Condition), Jason (Audience) will reduce his "out of area" behavior (see definition) (Behavior) to zero for four consecutive weeks (Degree).

Given what I know about Jason and his current baseline rate for "out of area," I decided to set the benchmarks at 25 percent intervals. Jason's baseline for "out of area" is an average of four times per day, and Benchmark 1 is met when the average drops to three times per day for two consecutive weeks. Benchmark 2 is met when the average drops to two, and so on. The last benchmark is simply a restatement of the annual goal.

I like using this method to identify and document behavior change. It is an easy way to collect and summarize data. The format stays the same for the entire year, which reduces confusion and complications later. This way, you can use different strategies and interventions to achieve the behavior change without having to collect data directly on the success of any one intervention. The strategies are working because Jason's aggression is decreasing. Why they work for this student becomes a qualitative observation on the part of the instructor. We don't have to answer "why" here. All we're interested in is the reduction of the problem behavior. Frankly, the classroom isn't a clinical environment. You can't control a lot of the extraneous variables, such as the presence or absence of another student that is a negative influence on our target kid, or an increase or decrease of home stability, and so on, and so forth. Much, much easier—the ultimate way to K.I.S.S.!

8

Less Can Be Better

Interval Recording and Time Sampling

Although counting and recording every event is the most exact method of data collection because it gives you a complete picture of the student with regard to the skill or behavior in question, it may be very inconvenient or actually impossible to record each and every time a behavior occurs. This could be due to the high frequency of the behavior, the long duration of a behavior, or because the student is in various settings throughout the day and therefore can't be observed reliably.

Interval Recording

Let's say you have a young student, Melissa, who presents some behavior challenges. She wanders around the room and bothers other students during instructional periods. She does this so frequently throughout the day that it is impossible to teach the class and collect data on her "out of area" behavior at the same time. In fact, the behavior can happen as much as once or twice a minute! (Note that Melissa's "out of area" behavior is much different from Jason's "out of area" behavior, described in Chapter 7.)

Since this happens when you are teaching, you ask a colleague—for example, an assistant, counselor, school psychologist, principal—to conduct an "interval recording" observation. Interval recording involves designating a short time period in a day—say, 10 or 15 minutes—in which the behavior will be directly observed and data will be collected. That time period is divided into minutes, and the minutes are divided into intervals a fixed number of seconds long. Intervals can be 5, 10, 15 seconds, or anything else you want. I use 10-second intervals because it makes it easy for me to keep track. During the 10-second interval, the observer places an *X* in the box on a recording form if the behavior is observed ANY TIME DURING THAT 10-SECOND INTERVAL.

In the case of Melissa, the observer sets a stop watch or timer and records whether Melisa is "out of area" according to the written behavior description ANY TIME during the first 10-second interval. So, if Melisa is "out of area" as soon as the interval starts, the observer marks an *X* and waits for the next interval to begin. If Melissa is in her seat throughout the entire 10-second interval, the observer marks an *O*. I have set up six intervals in each observation minute. If the entire observation period takes place in 15 minutes, there will be a total of 90 intervals. Therefore, there would be 90 data points. (Note: For a 10-minute observation period, there would be a total of 60 intervals, resulting in 60 data points.)

Since you have wisely chosen to sample Melissa's behavior because she is demonstrating "out of area" behavior so frequently throughout the day, you will want to take interval data in at least three DIFFERENT times of the school day—for example, morning, midday, and afternoon. This will allow you to use the average of the results as an estimate of Melissa's "out of area" behavior throughout the school day. If, however, you know that this "out of area" behavior occurs only during group instruction or independent work activities, take the data at these specific times and activities. (You may note that Melissa's behavior occurs more frequently in math than during reading time.)

Melissa's Out of Area Behavior

Description: Melissa is considered "out of area" when she is anywhere BUT where her teacher has told her to be (for example, out of her chair during independent seat work, off the carpet during story time, out of line when she's been asked to line up).

Start Time: Behavior starts when Melissa is not in her assigned area for 10 seconds or more.

Stop Time: Behavior stops when Melissa is in her assigned area for 10 seconds.

That's it. Figure 15 shows what Melissa's interval recording data look like.

It is best to report this kind of data as a "rate of behavior," or a percentage of the observation period. This way, if the length of any given observation period differs from that of another observation period, you can still compare the data accurately. Think of it this way: If you are able to complete a 15-minute observation on Melissa Tuesday morning, but Wednesday afternoon the observation was cut short by 5 minutes because she was given permission to go to the restroom, you can still compare the two observation sessions. To calculate the rate or percentage of intervals in which the behavior occurred, divide the number of intervals that Melissa was observed to be "out of area" by the total number of observation intervals. In this case, Melissa was observed to be "out of area" 34 out of the 90 observation intervals. That means her rate of "out of area" behavior was .377, or 38 percent of the designated observation.

Melissa's goal, then, could look like this:

> *During a designated observation period (Condition), Melissa (Audience) will decrease her "out of area"(see behavior description) (Behavior) to a rate of less than .10, or 10 percent, of designated observation intervals over three consecutive observation sessions (Degree).*

To evaluate progress, each week or so you have a colleague conduct an observation and take interval data to evaluate whether she is progressing toward mastering her goal.

FIGURE 15   Melissa's Interval Recording Data

Date: 2-15-10   Time: 11:15 to 11:30   10-second intervals

Minutes	Seconds					
	00	10	20	30	40	50
1	X	X	O	O	X	X
2	X	X	X	O	X	X
3	X	X	X	X	O	O
4	O	O	O	O	O	O
5	O	O	O	X	X	X
6	X	X	X	X	X	X
7	X	X	X	X	X	O
8	O	O	O	O	O	X
9	O	O	X	X	X	O
10	X	X	X	O	X	O
11	X	X	X	X	X	X
12	X	X	X	X	O	O
13	O	O	O	X	O	X
14	X	O	X	O	X	X
15	O	X	X	X	X	X
Totals	9	9	10	9	10	9

Number of intervals that "out of area" occurred: 56/90 = .622 or 62% out of area.

Time Sampling

Time sampling is a specific type of interval recording that can be used for high rates of behavior like Melissa's. The difference is in the length of the intervals and the total length of time in which the observation takes place. Instead of observing for a few minutes, such as 10 or 15 minutes at a time, you are actually observing a behavior over several hours. Each hour is divided into blocks of 10 or 15 minutes, not seconds. At the END of each interval, you observe whether the behavior is occurring at THAT TIME and mark the section on a recording form accordingly. With the typical interval recording just described, you indicate if the behavior occurred ANY TIME during the entire length of the designated interval. In time sampling, you only record whether the behavior is occurring at the very END of an interval. It is possible for a teacher to instruct and take time sample data at the same time. The advantage to this is that you don't have to rely on an outside observer.

Let's take another look at Melissa. Not only is she frequently out of her seat, she doesn't follow her teacher's directions. Check out this goal:

> *Melissa will follow teacher directions 85 percent of the time.*

Although writing an objective that reads this way is common, it's not very helpful. In the **A-B-C-D** format, you have the **A** (Audience: Melissa), and you have the **D** (Degree: 85 percent of the time). The **B** (Behavior: follow teacher directions) is not measurable! What does "following directions" mean? Does it mean she is doing what the rest of the class is doing? Does it mean she is following classroom rules? There's no way to know. Even if you did know, how would it be possible to count the number of directions a teacher gives during the day, let alone document whether Melissa followed them or not? If you can't do this, you can't get a true percentage, which means the **C** (Condition) and the **D** (Degree) don't work either. Anything you come up with will be C.R.A.P. data!

Suppose you decide to define "follow teacher directions" as "follow classroom rules." Okay, what are the classroom rules? Typically, classroom rules consist of something like this:

1. Keep hands and feet to yourself.
2. Raise your hand to speak.
3. Follow teacher directions.

This doesn't help much at all. The first and second rules may be observable, but they are context driven. In other words, depending on where and when, it may be perfectly fine to talk without raising a hand (for instance, at lunch time and during free time). Under certain circumstances, touching another person is considered appropriate (in gym class, for example, or during recess). The third rule means different things to different observers in different contexts. Therefore, it isn't measurable. You are right back where you started: C.R.A.P.

So, the first thing to do is define "follow teacher directions." I suggest something like this: "Follow directions" means "being in designated area, engaged in assigned task or activity, as directed by the teacher." This is okay because if the teacher is taking the data, he or she knows what following directions means at any given point of the day because he or she is the one who directs the activity. Collecting frequency data on this behavior is impossible, however, because counting the number of directions a teacher gives in any given period would be extremely difficult (too many) and the directions could vary from student to student. Even if you could do it, you wouldn't be able to do anything else. This calls for a carefully written **C** or condition statement so you not only know who and what you are looking for, you designate when you will be observing, too. You could rewrite the objective like this:

> *During designated observation periods (Condition),*
> *Melissa (Audience) will follow directions, defined as*
> *being in designated area, engaged in assigned task or*
> *activity, as directed by the teacher (Behavior) 85 percent*
> *of time observed (Degree).*

A time-sampling method of data collection is perfect for this goal. It's very easy to implement even when working with large groups of children. You set the timer for 10- or 15-minute intervals. When the timer goes off, you IMMEDIATELY look for Melissa to see if she is following directions, as you have defined it. If she is, you place an *O* in the appropriate section of the form (see Figure 16). If she isn't, you put an *X* in the section. After the observation period of one, two, or three hours, you then calculate a rate, just as we discussed previously: Summarize by counting the number of intervals that have an *X* and divide by the total number of intervals you observed to get a percentage of intervals during which Melissa was not following directions. This is very simple, and it gives you good data you CAN rely on.

FIGURE 16   Melissa's Time-Sampling Data

10-minute intervals per hour

	On the hour	10 min.	20 min.	30 min.	40 min.	50 min.
Hour 1	X	O	O	X	O	X
Hour 2	X	X	X	O	O	O
Hour 3	O	X	X	O	X	X

Number of intervals in which the behavior occurred: 10/24 (or .416). Melissa is "out of area" 42% of the designated observation period.

I can hear many of you out there protesting, "But this type of data collection doesn't capture all the problems I have with a youngster within the interval!" I understand that, but accuracy of data is ALWAYS better than impressions (in other words, C.R.A.P. data). Qualitative data, such as a brief narrative or observations, can supplement the quantitative data. Also, you may want to use a time-sampling approach but you can also add a few interval recordings to document the pervasive challenges throughout the day. Since it is difficult at times to get someone to take interval data frequently enough, combining these two similar approaches is advisable. However, the data summary must be done separately; the percentages cannot be combined because the format is totally different.

>✦✕✦<

In summary, with interval recording, you observe and note if the behavior occurs ANY time within the interval. With time sampling, you record the occurrence of the behavior only at the END of the interval. Because you're not recording every instance, these methods give you an ESTIMATE of the number of occurrences of the behavior, but an estimate is much more accurate than a "GUESSTIMATE." And it's convenient for a teacher to use these methods while engaging in instruction and working with larger groups of students.

9

Will This Never End?

Measuring Duration, Latency, and Intensity

To get a clear picture of a behavior, you often have to be able to measure duration (how long it takes to complete), latency (how long it takes to get started), and intensity (the force with which the behavior occurs).

Duration

When you are concerned with the amount of time it takes a youngster to complete a given activity, you should use duration recording. A good example of a situation where you need to record duration would be when a youngster who is in a vocational program needs to be able to assemble items for packaging at a specific rate of speed in order to be considered employable.

Here's another example: Timed math tests are used to measure how fluent and accurate a youngster is when using a math application such as addition, subtraction, multiplication, or division. Perhaps you have a fourth-grade student, Kory, who appears to have a solid understanding of these applications, but he is really slow. A typical fourth grader is expected to complete 20 problems in three minutes. Although Kory knows the facts, he is unable to meet this expectation. His baseline for completing 20 problems accurately is around eight minutes. In this case, you will need to record and analyze duration data. The data for Kory (Figure 17) can

FIGURE 17   Kory's Duration Data

Timed tests	1	2	3	4	5	6	7	8	9	10
Minutes to complete 20 problems	8	5	6	4	5	5.5	5	3.5	3.75	3.5

FIGURE 18   Graph of Kory's Duration Data

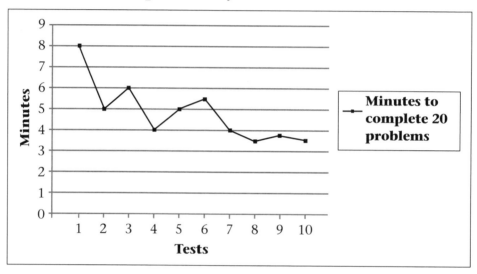

be graphed to present a visual picture of his progress (Figure 18). One look at a graph of this data shows that Kory is getting close to meeting the goal as written!

Latency

In other situations, the target behavior may reflect concern that a youngster takes too long to initiate a response when given a direction or presented a stimulus. This is called "latency." To collect data on this dimension of behavior, you identify three or four opportunities for a given response and record the actual total time it takes for the student to begin the task or begin to follow the direction.

Some years ago, I was asked to observe a third-grade student, Joey, who was not paying attention and failed to get his work completed. As a beginning intervention, the team reduced the amount of work he had to complete, but that strategy didn't seem to help. In fact, Joey was doing less and less. I observed him in a language arts class with 30 students. During the first part of the class, the teacher was presenting a lesson to the whole class. Joey was sitting up front, participating, and appeared to be engaged throughout the lesson. As the teacher was wrapping up and the class was transitioning to independent work, Joey very quietly cleared his desk with his arm, allowing papers, books, pencils, and everything else to drop to the floor. After the other students began their work, Joey spent the next 13 minutes rearranging his materials and desk. He did this very quietly and in a way that was not disruptive. The teacher hardly noticed him. She was too busy monitoring 29 other kids. By the time he began his seat work, the class period was over. In other words, the behavioral dimension of concern at this point was latency: the average amount of time it took Joey to begin his work. After several other observations, the teacher was shocked to realize that 12 to 15 minutes was the typical amount of time it took Joey to start his work. Figures 19 and 20 show the raw data and the data graphed.

Intensity

Intensity is a very difficult behavioral dimension to quantify. However, teachers frequently see a reduction in behavioral intensity, such as the force a student uses during an aggressive outburst, before the frequency of the behavior is reduced. I have used a scale like the one I'll describe next to help staff capture this dimension in a quasi-quantifiable way. However, these data should be interpreted with great caution, as they reflect a subjective rather than

FIGURE 19   Joey's Latency Data

Observations	1	2	3	4	5
Minutes before task initiation	10	12	11	7	9

FIGURE 20   Graph of Joey's Latency Data

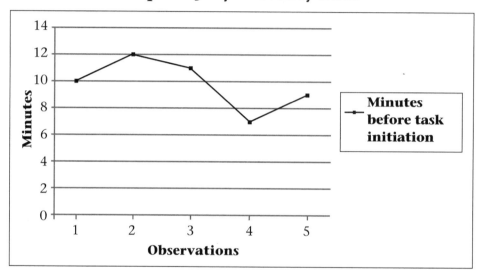

an objective evaluation. If you're not careful, you'll end up with more work and C.R.A.P. data.

I suggest using a three-point scale to describe intensity or force: 1 = low intensity, 2 = medium intensity, and 3 = high intensity, or with significant force. There should never be partial ratings such as 1.5, 2.5, and so on. Each number needs to have a clear behavioral anchor or description and an example so that multiple observers would rate the intensity as similarly as possible. These anchors or descriptions are based upon the individual student and the student's unique manifestation of the behavior. For example, let's think about Randi, a youngster who experiences severe communication challenges and uses physical aggression to escape academic demands. When she is mildly upset, she is likely to slap at an adult with an open hand one time, making contact with the adult's body in some fashion. However, the slap does not leave a mark, nor does it hurt the adult. This type of physical aggression for this youngster could be considered a 1, or low intensity aggression. In another situation, however, the same youngster may slap at an adult with an open hand more than one time in succession, and the adult may feel some discomfort. This example would rate a 2, or medium intensity. Unfortunately, there are some occasions this youngster may hit an adult with a closed fist multiple times and bite or kick, leaving marks and causing pain to the adult. This would rate a 3, or high intensity.

Figures 21 and 22 demonstrate how you would collect the data and graph it in a meaningful way. Figure 21 provides a total of the frequency of the behavior each week and an average of the intensity rating for the week. Through the graph in Figure 22, you can see that the numbers of aggressive incidents are still quite high, but the intensity of each incident has been reduced. By Week 10, all of the 10 incidents are rated as low. However, the number has not decreased. If the goal is to decrease the total number of incidents, you could define the behavior DISCRETELY enough to include only serious infractions—what you now consider to be a 3, or high intensity. If you had, you would have reduced the incidents, defined by the level of intensity only, significantly. If you want to evaluate intensity, then be sure that the criteria refer to reduction of intensity and do not include frequency.

FIGURE 21   Randi's Intensity Data

	Week									
	1	2	3	4	5	6	7	8	9	10
Number of aggressive outbursts	8	7	9	7	9	8	6	8	9	7
Average intensity rating for the week	2.89	2.5	2.1	1.5	1.2	1.6	1.3	.5	.35	.2

FIGURE 22   Graph of Randi's Intensity Data

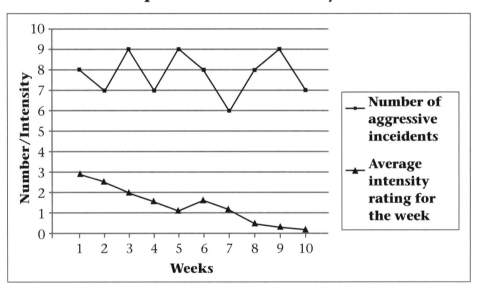

10

Are We There Yet?

Data Collection and Beyond

The type of data you choose to measure the frequency of a behavior is directly related to how the goal or objective is written. Be sure not to include two different dimensions to measure in one goal. However, you CAN have an annual goal with different objectives written to measure multiple dimensions. For instance, frequency of aggression could be addressed in one objective, and intensity of aggression addressed in another. I'm not necessarily recommending that . . . too complicated for me, but it can be done.

Figure 23 is a chart to help you decide, when you are trying to decrease a challenging behavior, which frequency data you should choose to evaluate progress.

Who Should Be Taking Data?

The answer to this question is EVERYONE WHO CAN! The teacher is an obvious answer in a self-contained classroom or resource room, or in an inclusion setting when team teaching occurs. But there are many others who can help. If paraprofessionals are available, this duty could be assigned to them. When using an interval recording format, an outside observer must pitch in. You could solicit the support of administrative staff, counselors, school psychologists, speech and language pathologists, student teachers—and anyone else you can think of. In some cases, when

FIGURE 23   Decreasing Behavior: Which Data Collection System to Use

Choose This	Under These Circumstances
Scatter Plot	Behavior has a clear "Start" and "Stop" time and occurs less than once in 15–30 minutes. Students may travel from one setting to another and several adults must be responsible for data collection.
Interval Sample	Behavior occurs at a high frequency, or continuously, and a third-party observer is available to take data. Several data samples should be taken across different contexts and times of day.
Time Sample	Behavior occurs at least once in 15 minutes and the teacher must collect the data while instructing others.
Duration Recording	Concerns relate to how long a behavior occurs once it starts.
Latency Recording	Concerns relate to how long it takes the student to initiate a task, begin to follow a direction, etc.

you are evaluating a student's response to intervention, you would assign data collection to the general education teacher, particularly when using the time-sampling method. Students can also collect data on themselves with teachers doing periodic reliability checks. Remember, whether you realize it or not, general education teachers shoulder as much responsibility for a student's progress as do special education teachers. Regardless, collecting data is a team responsibility.

I often meet teachers who are a bit, shall we say, "obsessive-compulsive." These are the folks who believe they could never delegate any sort of responsibility to another staff person (even their own teaching assistants). They tell me they can't trust anyone else to do a proper job. These teachers are also the people who complain nonstop about how overwhelmed and overworked they are. When I visit some classrooms, I can tell immediately I have met such a teacher; their assistants are generally talking to each other, sitting doing nothing, or cutting out pictures! Use your resources wisely.

Delegating data collection is possible if the objective is written clearly, in **A-B-C-D** format, and has all the information needed—in other words, if the objective is self-contained. It is easy to train paraprofessionals. The **C** or condition statement identifies where and when the youngster is expected to perform. The people who are present at that time are all potential data collectors. If you have followed my advice, you will have identified how you will collect data when you write your objectives. Handing off the data collection duty to others should be relatively easy, with just a little bit of direction and periodic check-ups.

So, who should be taking data? Everybody!

How Frequently Must Data Be Taken?

Most of you won't like my answer to this question, which is "as often as possible." First of all, the goals and objectives, written in **A-B-C-D** format, give you a clue. Are you grading products or observing behavior? Product grades are no-brainers . . . use all of them. Collecting observational data is quite another story. Take another look at Figure 23: Which dimension of behavior—frequency, duration, latency, or intensity—are you seeking to change?

The more data points the better. However, the data MUST be accurate. When using controlled presentations as an instructional strategy, it is relatively easy to take data daily several times a week.

This is possible because the data sheet becomes your lesson plan and helps to establish instructional consistency. The more opportunities the student has to demonstrate the desired behavior, the more data points there should be.

If you are seeking to reduce a challenging behavior, the frequency of data collection depends on the dimension you are observing. If a behavior occurs no more than once or twice an hour and only lasts a few seconds, an accurate recording of each occurrence is wise. If the behavior occurs so frequently that it is impossible to record each event (in other words, high rates of behavior, occurring more than once per minute), take "data probes" or samples once each week in order to assess whether the behavior is decreasing, using an interval recording format or time sampling. Since you are likely to serve several students on IEPs, designate certain days to collect specific types of behavior. Make it as routine as possible. Data collection should not be an additional responsibility; it should be a direct outcome of completing instruction.

How Should Data Be Used?

Taking good data is really only the first step. Data collection must result in some type of summary so that the numbers can be reviewed and analyzed. Data analysis ultimately leads to decisions about whether instructional strategies are progressing adequately or objectives need to be modified. Raw data alone are not useful, often because there is just too much information. To be meaningful, raw data need to be reduced to reflect a typical performance of the skill, such as an average per week or month, a percentage correct, a rate of performance, and so forth.

Once raw data are reduced or summarized into expressions of typical performance, they can be presented to all members of the IEP team for review. You know the saying "A picture is worth a thousand words." This can't be truer than in the case of expressing data in meaningful ways to a group of people. Drawing a picture of the data summaries, or graphing data, simplifies this process greatly. It becomes a lasting picture, if you will, of how effective the instruction has been or hasn't been. It is a "thing" that you can hold in your hand. It is a permanent artifact of instruction that is a critical component of any defensible education program.

When you have that picture, a new set of questions becomes necessary. Remember my example in Chapter 2 about driving from Cleveland to Washington, DC? Your destination, or annual goal, remains constant. HOW you get there, the route and directions you use, are more flexible, depending on whether you encounter detours, construction, or unexpected stops along the way. So now you have some data about the routes you initially chose to meet the ultimate goal. What do these data, or experiences, tell you? Is the weather so lousy that you prefer to fly?

In other words, once the data are collected and translated into a visual summary, you must ask a new question about your choice of instructional strategies: Do you continue on the same route toward accomplishing the annual goal or not? Are the instructional strategies you have chosen appropriate for this student? What needs to change, if anything, in order for the student to meet the chosen goals?

The whole purpose of writing measurable goals and taking reliable data is to use that data to assess the effectiveness of instruction. In other words, is WHAT you teach and HOW you teach it working? If you haven't got the message by now, the bottom line is this:

Are kids learning or not?

In today's educational world, if kids are learning, prove it! If you can't prove it, they aren't learning. You can argue with me until you're blue in the face, but proof in the form of some quantifiable measurement is absolutely necessary.

For each goal, data collection is more than generating colorful graphs—the graphs need to be studied and interpreted regularly to see if instruction is working. If the youngster is making reasonable progress, the message is "continue as planned." However, if the youngster is NOT making progress, or if progress is extremely slow, it is the teachers' responsibility to make adjustments in strategies and methodologies in order to increase the student's learning. We are being held accountable for just that: making SURE a student progresses through the curriculum. The final kicker is that our decisions about altering instruction to increase learning MUST BE ONGOING. For the most part, waiting nine weeks (a typical grading period) to evaluate the effectiveness of a strategy or behavior plan will not be sufficient. Monitoring progress on a weekly or biweekly basis is likely to be the norm.

How in the World Can I Make This Work?

To quote myself from Chapter 1, how you collect data depends upon two equally important factors:

1. The clarity and completeness of the goals and objectives you write

2. The convenience and practicality of the data collection systems you choose

I cannot emphasize enough how important convenience is. Not only must the collection methods be easy, summarizing the data into meaningful graphs is even more important. Teachers tell me that one of the biggest challenges they face is keeping up with graphing and data summarization. What that means to me is this: Teachers are not evaluating the effectiveness of their intervention strategies on a regular basis. More often than not, once again they are relying on their impressions of progress. You already know how I feel about that—C.R.A.P.! Your impressions and $4.85 can get me a Starbuck's cup of coffee. This approach isn't defensible, and it isn't accountable.

My caution here is not to overload your systems. Ask yourself, "What is it that I need to keep track of? What data will be descriptive of progress?" That's what you record—nothing more, nothing less. The beauty of the **A-B-C-D** format is that the objectives are self-contained: They tell you whose behavior needs to be changed, what behavior is to be changed, where and when and under what conditions you need to measure that behavior, and what is considered to be mastery.

Finally, ladies and gentlemen, let me leave you with THE most important point of all: K.I.S.S.—Keep It Simple Sweetheart!

Appendix A

Increasing Behavior Examples

This appendix includes goals and objectives for three students who need to increase a desirable behavior. The goals and objectives are written in the **A-B-C-D** format, and examples are provided of the data collected and method of collecting it.

Example 1: Carol

1. Upon teacher request (Condition), Carol (Audience) will verbally state her first and last name, her address, and her telephone number including area code (Behavior) 5/5 designated opportunities over two consecutive weeks (Degree).

    a. Upon teacher request (Condition), Carol (Audience) will state her first and last name (Behavior) 5/5 designated opportunities (Degree).

    b. Upon teacher request (Condition), Carol (Audience) will state her complete address, including street number, street name, city, state, and zip code (Behavior) 5/5 designated opportunities (Degree).

    c. Upon teacher request (Condition), Carol (Audience) will state her telephone number, including area code (Behavior) 5/5 designated opportunities (Degree).

    d. Upon teacher request (Condition), Carol (Audience) will state her first and last name, her address, and her telephone number, including area code (Behavior) 5/5 designated opportunities over two consecutive weeks (Degree).

The teacher adapted the Self-Graphing Data Form (Appendix C, p. 93) to collect data for Carol. As you can see, Carol is progressing slowly toward goal mastery.

Self-Graphing Data Form for Carol

Dates

Items	9/15	9/30	10/15	10/30	11/15	11/30	12/15	12/30	1/15	1/30	2/15	2/28	3/15	3/30	4/15
Phone number	✗	✗	✗	✗	✗	✗	✗	✗	✗	✗	✗	✗	8	8	[8]
Zip code	✗	✗	✗	✗	✗	✗	✗	✗	✗	✗	[7]	[7]	[✗]	[✗]	7
State	6	6	6	6	6	6	6	[6]	6	[6]	6	6	6	6	6
City	5	5	5	5	[5]	5	[5]	5	5	5	5	5	5	5	5
Street name	[4]	[✗]	[✗]	[✗]	4	[4]	4	4	[✗]	4	4	4	4	4	4
Street number	✗	✗	✗	✗	3	3	3	3	3	3	3	3	3	3	3
Last name	2	2	2	2	2	2	2	2	2	2	2	2	2	2	2
First name	1	1	1	1	1	1	1	1	1	1	1	1	1	1	1
Session	1	2	3	4	5	6	7	8	9	10	11	12	13	14	15

Example 2: Max

1. During the final quarter of the school year (Condition), Max (Audience) will attend school (Behavior) 95% of scheduled school days (Degree).

   a. During the first quarter of the school year (Condition), Max (Audience) will attend school (Behavior) 75% of scheduled school days (Degree).

   b. During the second quarter of the school year (Condition), Max (Audience) will attend school (Behavior) 85% of scheduled school days (Degree).

   c. During the third quarter of the school year (Condition), Max (Audience) will attend school (Behavior) 90% of scheduled school days (Degree).

   d. During the final quarter of the school year (Condition), Max (Audience) will attend school (Behavior) 95% of scheduled school days (Degree).

   This goal and related objectives call for permanent product data—specifically, information from quarterly school attendance records. The teacher obtained this information and graphed it to provide strong visual representation of the data for both Max and his family.

Max's School Attendance Data

	Quarter 1	Quarter 2	Quarter 3	Quarter 4
Percentage of days present	71%	80%	89%	96%
Target	75%	85%	90%	95%

Graph of Max's School Attendance Data

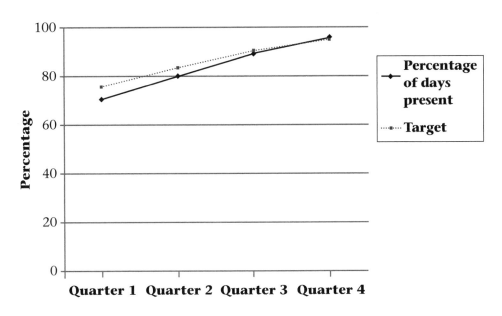

Example 3: Daniel

1. When presented with third-grade level sight words (Condition), Daniel (Audience) will read out loud a list of 100 words (Behavior) with no errors 5/5 designated opportunities over two consecutive weeks (Degree).

   a. When presented with the first 25 third-grade level sight words (Condition), Daniel (Audience) will read the words out loud from the list (Behavior) with no errors by October 25, 2010 (Degree).

   b. When presented with the next 25 third-grade level sight words (Condition), Daniel (Audience) will read the words out loud from the list (Behavior) with no errors by December 15, 2010 (Degree).

   c. When presented with the next 25 third-grade level sight words (Condition), Daniel (Audience) will read the words out loud from the list (Behavior) with no errors by February 1, 2011 (Degree).

   d. When presented with all 100 third-grade level sight words (Condition), Daniel (Audience) will read the words out loud from the list (Behavior) with no errors by May 15, 2011 (Degree).

   > *As with Carol, the teacher collected data on Daniel's goal and associated objectives on an adapted version of the Self-Graphing Data Form (Appendix C, p. 93), as shown. This graph represents Daniel's progress on the second set of third-grade sight words.*

Self-Graphing Data Form for Daniel

Items	11/1	11/2	11/4	11/5	11/7	11/8	11/9	11/14	11/15	11/18
					Dates					
knew	25	25	25	25	25	25	25	25	25	25
very	24	24	24	24	24	24	24	24	24	24
right	23	23	23	23	23	23	23	23	23	23
about	22	22	22	22	22	22	22	22	22	22
would	21	21	21	21	21	21	21	21	21	21
once	20	20	20	20	20	20	20	20	20	20
know	19	19	19	19	19	19	19	19	19	19
live	18	18	18	18	18	18	18	18	18	18
open	17	17	17	17	17	17	17	17	17	17
over	16	16	16	16	16	16	16	16	16	16
put	15	15	15	15	15	15	15	15	15	15
round	14	14	14	14	14	14	14	14	14	14
going	13	13	13	13	13	13	13	13	13	13
every	12	12	12	12	12	12	12	12	12	12
thank	11	11	11	11	11	11	11	11	11	11
them	10	10	10	10	10	10	10	10	10	10
stop	9	9	9	9	9	9	9	9	9	9
take	8	8	8	8	8	8	8	8	8	8
then	7	7	7	7	7	7	7	7	7	7
could	6	6	6	6	6	6	6	6	6	6
ask	5	5	5	5	5	5	5	5	5	5
old	4	4	4	4	4	4	4	4	4	4
some	3	3	3	3	3	3	3	3	3	3
how	2	2	2	2	2	2	2	2	2	2
who	1	1	1	1	1	1	1	1	1	1
Session	1	2	3	4	5	6	7	8	9	10
No. correct	10	9	15	16	17	18	18	18	20	21

Appendix B

Decreasing Behavior Examples

This appendix includes goals and objectives for three students who need to decrease a challenging behavior. The goals and objectives are written in the **A-B-C-D** format, and examples are provided of the data collected and method of collecting it.

Remember, you need to define the behaviors you wish to reduce or eliminate carefully. In addition to a behavior description that is clearly measurable, you must include a "Start" and "Stop" time. Without them, the data will be unreliable. Finally, a baseline rate must be included in order for goals to be clear.

Molly's Target Behavior: Aggression

Description

"Physical aggression" is defined as hitting, kicking, or otherwise inflicting physical harm upon another individual to such a degree as to cause pain, bruising, or significant injury.

Start/Stop Time

"Physical aggression" is considered to start at the point that Molly runs after the person she targets, swings at another person, or otherwise indicates she is going to strike another person. The behavior is considered to be stopped when she is no longer physically aggressive and has been following her scheduled activities for one hour or more.

Baseline Rate

Once per week

Goals and Objectives

1. Throughout the school day (Condition), Molly (Audience) will reduce physical aggression, defined as hitting, kicking, or otherwise inflicting physical harm upon another individual to such a degree as to cause pain, bruising, or significant injury (Behavior) to zero for four consecutive weeks (Degree).

    a. Throughout the school day (Condition), Molly (Audience) will reduce physical aggression, defined as hitting, kicking, or otherwise inflicting physical harm upon another individual to such a degree as to cause pain, bruising, or significant injury (Behavior), to one or less for two consecutive weeks by November 30, 2011 (Degree).

    b. Throughout the school day (Condition), Molly (Audience) will reduce physical aggression, defined as hitting, kicking, or otherwise inflicting physical harm upon another individual, to such a degree as to cause pain, bruising, or significant injury (Behavior) to one or less for three consecutive weeks by January 30, 2012 (Degree).

    c. Throughout the school day (Condition), Molly (Audience) will reduce physical aggression, defined as hitting, kicking, or otherwise inflicting physical harm upon another individual, to such a degree as to cause pain, bruising, or significant injury (Behavior) to one or less for four consecutive weeks by March 1, 2012 (Degree).

    d. Throughout the school day (Condition), Molly (Audience) will reduce physical aggression, defined as hitting, kicking, or otherwise inflicting physical harm upon another individual to such a degree as to cause pain, bruising, or significant injury (Behavior), to zero for four consecutive weeks by June 1, 2012 (Degree).

Because Molly's behavior is fairly infrequent, the teacher can use a Scatter Plot Data Form (Appendix C, p. 96), recording instances of the behavior while still teaching. The data for Molly's aggressive behavior for the first week of intervention suggest there may be some concern because her aggressive outbursts occurred twice during the week, representing a significant increase over baseline. However, the team should continue the interventions as planned for at least one more week in order to determine whether they will be successful over time.

Scatter Plot Data Form for Molly

Class/activity	Mon.	Tue.	Wed.	Thurs.	Fri.
Math block					
Math block					
Specials					
Written expression		X			
Lunch					
Language arts block					X
Science					
World history					
TOTAL Xs		1			1

Jay's Target Behavior: Off Task

Description

"Off task" is defined as any behavior exhibited that is not related to assigned task or activity (e.g., talking with peers, disrupting peer activities, playing with materials, not listening to the teacher, approaching the teacher and asking questions when explicitly directed to an assigned area, wandering the room, leaving the classroom, etc.).

Start/Stop Times

"Off task" behavior begins when any of the above description occurs and ends when Jay is engaged in the assigned task or activity for three minutes or more.

Baseline Rate

Jay was observed to be "off task" 51/90 intervals observed, or 56% of the observation period.

Objective and Goals

1. During designated observation periods (Condition), Jay (Audience) will reduce "off task" behavior, defined as any behavior exhibited that is not related to assigned task or activity (Behavior), to less than 10% in 3/4 designated observation periods (Degree).

   a. During designated observation periods (Condition), Jay (Audience) will reduce "off task" behavior, defined as any behavior exhibited that is not related to assigned task or activity (Behavior), to less than 30% in 3/4 designated observation periods by December 1, 2010 (Degree).

   b. During designated observation periods (Condition), Jay (Audience) will reduce "off task" behavior, defined as any behavior exhibited that is not related to assigned task or activity (Behavior) to less than 20% in 3/4 designated observation periods by March 1, 2011 (Degree).

c. During designated observation periods (Condition), Jay (Audience) will reduce "off task" behavior, defined as any behavior exhibited that is not related to assigned task or activity (Behavior), to less than 10% in 3/4 designated observation periods by June 1, 2011 (Degree).

Since Jay's behavior occurs at a very high rate, the teacher asked a colleague to take interval data, observing for 15 minutes and noting every 10 seconds whether the behavior occurred during that time frame. The observer used the Interval Data Form (Appendix C, p. 94). The data, taken in January, indicate that Jay is well on his way to meeting his annual goal by June.

Interval Data Form for Jay

Minutes	Seconds					
	0	**10**	**20**	**30**	**40**	**50**
1	O	O	O	O	O	O
2	O	O	O	O	O	O
3	X	O	O	O	O	O
4	O	O	O	O	O	O
5	O	O	X	X	X	O
6	O	O	X	O	O	O
7	X	X	O	O	O	O
8	O	O	O	O	O	O
9	O	O	O	O	O	O
10	O	O	O	O	O	O
11	O	O	O	O	O	O
12	O	X	X	X	O	O
13	O	O	O	O	O	O
14	O	O	X	X	X	X
15	O	O	O	O	O	O
TOTAL Xs	2	2	4	3	2	1

Rate of behavior 14/90 or 16%

Tom's Target Behavior: Defiance/Disrespect

Description

"Defiance/disrespect" is defined as refusing to complete an activity or follow an academic direction (for example, walking around the room, poking at peers, ripping up work tasks, hiding under his desk, making inappropriate noises, throwing items, arguing and teasing, making statements such as "You can't make me do it," "You're not my teacher," "No," "I hate you," whining, and so on). On rare occasions, behavior will escalate to uncontrollable crying or negative statements such as "I hate this—I don't want to be alive."

Start/Stop Times

The behavior starts when Tom refuses to follow a specific teacher direction within 60 seconds and/or begins making negative and inappropriate comments to the teacher. The behavior stops when he is engaged in a specified activity for at least 5 minutes.

Baseline Rate

During baseline observation, the behavior was observed five out of eight 15-minute intervals in a two-hour time sample. Rate equals .625, or 63% of designated observation intervals.

Goal and Objectives

1. During designated observation periods (Condition), Tom (Audience) will reduce "defiance/disrespect," defined as refusing to complete an activity or follow an academic direction (for example, walking around the room, poking at peers, ripping up work tasks, hiding under his desk, making inappropriate noises, throwing items, arguing and teasing making statements such as "You can't make me do it," "You're not my teacher," "No," "I hate you"), whining, and so on (Behavior) to zero for two

consecutive observations (Degree). *Note:* On rare occasions, behavior will escalate to uncontrollable crying, or negative statements such as "I hate this, I don't want to be alive."

a. During designated observation periods (Condition), Tom (Audience) will reduce "defiance/disrespect," defined as refusing to complete an activity or follow an academic direction (for example, walking around the room, poking at peers, ripping up work tasks, hiding under his desk, making inappropriate noises, throwing items, arguing and teasing, making statements such as "You can't make me do it," "You're not my teacher," "No," "I hate you"), whining, and so on (Behavior) to a rate of .375 or 38% of designated observation intervals for two consecutive observations (Degree) by October 30, 2010. *Note:* On rare occasions, Behavior will escalate to uncontrollable crying or negative statements such as "I hate this, I don't want to be alive."

b. During designated observation periods (Condition), Tom (Audience) will reduce "defiance/disrespect," defined as refusing to complete an activity or follow an academic direction (for example, walking around the room, poking at peers, ripping up work tasks, hiding under his desk, making inappropriate noises, throwing items, arguing and teasing, making statements such as "You can't make me do it," "You're not my teacher," "No," "I hate you"), whining, and so on (Behavior) to a rate of .25 or 25% of designated observation intervals for two consecutive observations (Degree) by January 15, 2011. On rare occasions, behavior will escalate to uncontrollable crying, negative statements such as "I hate this, I don't want to be alive."

c. During designated observation periods (Condition), Tom (Audience) will reduce "defiance/disrespect," defined as refusing to complete an activity or follow an academic direction (for example, walking around the room, poking at peers, ripping up work tasks, hiding under his desk, making inappropriate noises, throwing items, arguing and teasing, making statements such as "You can't make me do it," "You're not my teacher," "No," "I hate you"), whining, and so on (Behavior) to a rate of .125 or 13% of designated observation intervals for two consecutive observations (Degree) by April 1, 2011. *Note:* On rare occasions, behavior will escalate to uncontrollable crying or negative statements such as "I hate this, I don't want to be alive."

d. During designated observation periods (Condition), Tom (Audience) will reduce "defiance/disrespect," defined as refusing to complete an activity or follow an academic direction (for example, walking around the room, poking at peers, ripping up work tasks, hiding under his desk, making inappropriate noises, throwing items, arguing and teasing, making statements such as "You can't make me do it," "You're not my teacher," "No," "I hate you"), whining, and so on (Behavior) to zero for 2 consecutive observations (Degree) by June 1, 2011. *Note:* On rare occasions, behavior will escalate to uncontrollable crying, negative statements such as "I hate this, I don't want to be alive."

Tom's behavior is also occurring at a very high rate, and so a scatter plot collection method wouldn't be possible. The baseline therefore was taken using the time-sampling approach. This way, the teacher could take responsibility for collecting the data but still teach while doing so. To use this approach, the teacher designated two hours during a specific day to collect data. The teacher divided that 2-hour time period into 15-minute intervals and set a timer. When the timer went off, the teacher immediately looked at Tom and recorded whether he was demonstrating the target behavior AT THAT MOMENT.

The teacher then divided the number of intervals the behavior was observed by the total number of intervals in the observation period. The teacher used the Time-Sampling Data Form (Appendix C, p. 95).

Time-Sampling Data Form for Tom

Minutes

Hours	0	15	30	45
1	O	X	O	O
2	O	O	X	X
TOTAL Xs	O	1	1	1

Rate of behavior 3/8 or 38%

Appendix C

Reproducible Data Collection Forms

The forms included in this section can and should be modified to meet your individual needs.

- The *Self-Graphing Data Form* provides room for 10 items, but this same approach is appropriate for 20, 50, or even 100 items, as needed.

- The *Interval Data Form* is set up for a 15-minute observation period, but there is no reason that the same form couldn't be used for a 10-minute period. It works because you are calculating the rate or percentage of intervals the behavior is observed. Therefore, you can easily compare the percentage of intervals when you have conducted 15, 10, or even 12-minute observations.

- The same is true for the *Time-Sampling Data Form*. Instead of using 10 seconds (for interval recording) or 10 minutes (for time-sampling intervals), it may be more appropriate to divide the entire observation into 15-second or 15-minute sections.

- The *Scatter Plot Data Form* is easy to adapt as well. Under "Class/activity," you can list anything you like—you could also add columns for Saturday and Sunday if parents are collecting data over the weekend.

Self-Graphing Data Form Directions

"Items" refer to the steps, parts, activities, or tasks that are required to master the goal. List all the required items from first to last, bottom to top. At the top of the grid, note the date of the observation. During designated observation periods, indicate that the student is successful performing the task by circling the number in the appropriate column to the right of the item. If the student is not successful, place an X on that step. Once the session is over, count the number of circles. Place a square on the numeral representing the number of correct responses. Connect the squares to form a graph of the student's progress.

Self-Graphing Data Form

Student _____

Goal _____

Dates _____

Dates

Items																	
	10	10	10	10	10	10	10	10	10	10	10	10	10	10	10	10	10
	9	9	9	9	9	9	9	9	9	9	9	9	9	9	9	9	8
	8	8	8	8	8	8	8	8	8	8	8	8	8	8	8	8	8
	7	7	7	7	7	7	7	7	7	7	7	7	7	7	7	7	7
	6	6	6	6	6	6	6	6	6	6	6	6	6	6	6	6	6
	5	5	5	5	5	5	5	5	5	5	5	5	5	5	5	5	5
	4	4	4	4	4	4	4	4	4	4	4	4	4	4	4	4	4
	3	3	3	3	3	3	3	3	3	3	3	3	3	3	3	3	3
	2	2	2	2	2	2	2	2	2	2	2	2	2	2	2	2	2
	1	1	1	1	1	1	1	1	1	1	1	1	1	1	1	1	1
Session																	

Comments _____

From *Data Without Tears: How to Write Measurable Goals and Collect Meaningful Data*, © 2010 by Terri Chiara Johnston, Champaign, IL: Research Press (800-519-2707, www.researchpress.com)

Interval Data Form

Student ______________________________ Date ______________

Behavior description ______________________________

____

____

____

	Seconds: 0	10	20	30	40	50
Minutes 1						
2						
3						
4						
5						
6						
7						
8						
9						
10						
11						
12						
13						
14						
15						
TOTAL Xs						

Rate of behavior ______________________________

Rate = number of intervals the behavior was observed divided by the total number of observation intervals.

Comments ______________________________

____

Time-Sampling Data Form

Student _____ Date _____

Behavior description _____

_____

_____

_____

Minutes

	0	10	20	30	40	50
1						
2						
3						
TOTAL Xs						

Hours

Rate of behavior _____

Rate = number of intervals the behavior was observed divided by the total number of observation intervals.

Comments _____

_____

Scatter Plot Data Form

Record each occurrence of the target behavior by day and class/actvity. Total the number of occurrences each day and calculate an average for the day or week.

Student _____   Dates _____

Behavior description _____

Start and Stop Time _____

Class/activity	Monday	Tuesday	Wednesday	Thursday	Friday
TOTALS					

Comments _____

From *Data Without Tears: How to Write Measurable Goals and Collect Meaningful Data*, © 2010 by Terri Chiara Johnston, Champaign, IL: Research Press (800-519-2707, www.researchpress.com)

References and Bibliography

Asher, S. L., Gordon, S. B., Selbst, M. C., & Cooperberg, M. (2010). *The behavior problems resource kit: Forms and procedures for identification, measurement, and intervention.* Champaign, IL: Research Press.

Alberto, P. A., & Troutman, A. C. (1999). *Applied behavior analysis for teachers* (5th ed.). Upper Saddle River, NJ: Prentice Hall.

Bateman, B. D. (2007). *From gobbledygook to clearly written annual IEP goals.* Verona, WI: Attainment Company.

Bateman, B. D., & Golly, A. (2003). *Why Johnny doesn't behavior: Twenty tips and measurable BIPs.* Verona, WI: Attainment Company.

Bateman, B. D., & Herr, C. M. (2006). *Writing measurable IEP goals and objectives.* Verona, WI: Attainment Company.

Bateman, B. D., & Linden, M. A. (2006). *Better IEPs: How to develop legally correct and educationally useful programs* (4th ed.). Verona, WI: Attainment Company.

Courtade-Little, G., & Browder, D. M. (2005). *Aligning IEPs to academic standards: For students with moderate and severe disabilities.* Verona, WI: Attainment Company.

McDougal, J. L., Chafouleas, S. M., & Waterman, B. (2006). *Functional behavioral assessment and interventions in schools: A practitioner's guide.* Champaign, IL: Research Press.

Melograno, V. (2002). *Train the trainer certificate program: How adults learn and how to design and evaluate effective training.* Unpublished manuscript, Cleveland State University, Division of Continuing Education.

Wright, J. (2007). *RTI toolkit: A practical guide for schools.* Port Chester, NY: Dude Publishing.

About the Author

A graduate of Kent State University, Terri Chiara Johnston, Ph.D., has worked with challenging students for more than 30 years. She has extensive training in applied behavior analysis, structured teaching (TEACCH), and crisis management. Terri was a teacher, school psychologist, and program director/principal prior to retiring from the public schools in 2005. A recognized expert in the area of autism and emotional disturbance, she is currently CEO of Support 4 Teachers (www.support4teachers.com), an organization providing educational consulting and professional training. In her role as adjunct faculty for Ashland University, Terri is exploring the possibilities of web-based consultation and training opportunities for teachers across the country. A sought-after speaker, she draws on her colorful experience to provide her listeners with insights and knowledge that can be applied immediately, giving them an opportunity to reclaim their power to make a difference in their students' lives.

Terri and her staff are available for consultation, speaking engagements, and workshops.

Support4Teachers
P.O. Box 436 • Avon, Ohio 44011
Web: www.support4teachers.com
Phone: (440) 666–7985
E-mail: info@support4teachers.com